Concert and Contest COLLECTION

Compiled and Edited by H. VOXMAN

 for

Bb BASS CLARINET with piano accompaniment

C O N T E N T S

HAL•LEONARD CORPORATION
7777 W. BLUEMOUND RD. P.O. BOX 13819 MILWAUKEE, WI 53213

Sarabande and Bourrée
from First French Suite

J. S. BACH
Transcribed by R. Hervig

Patrol Russe

V. VOLOSCHINOV
Transcribed by H. Voxman

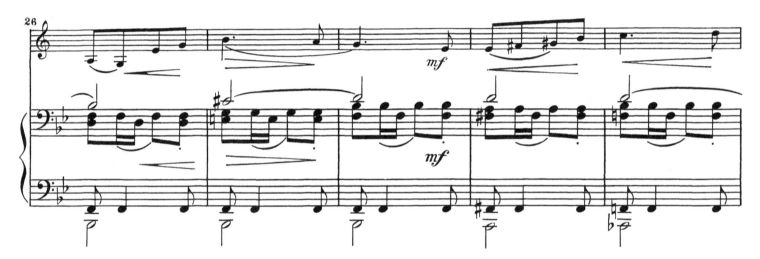

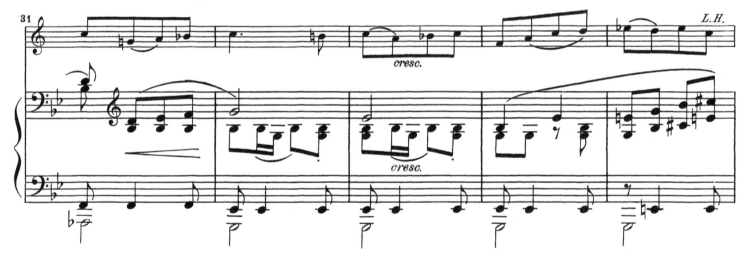

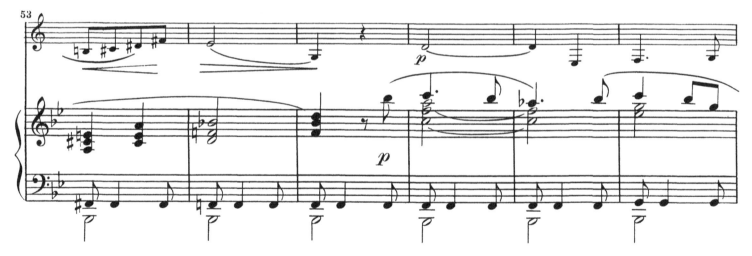

Mosaic

R. H. WALTHEW
Transcribed by H. Voxman

Largo and Allegro Vivace
from Sonata in Bb Major

J. B. LOEILLET
Transcribed by H. Voxman

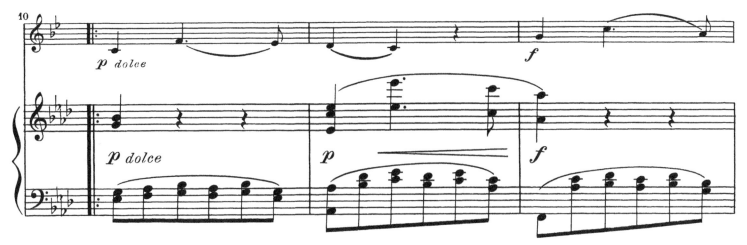

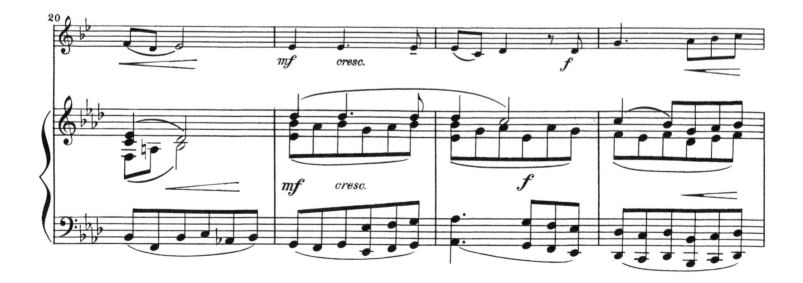

Two Russian Pieces

V. KALINIKOFF
Transcribed by H. Voxman

I - LAMENT

II - SCHERZO

V. KOSSENKO
Transcribed by H. Voxman

Concerto No. 8 in Bb

G. F. HANDEL
Transcribed by H. Voxman

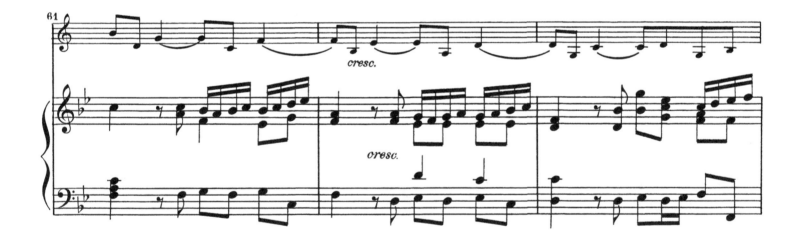

Largo and Allegro
from Sonata I, Op. 3

Realization by
R. Hervig

J. B. LOEILLET
Transcribed by H. Voxman

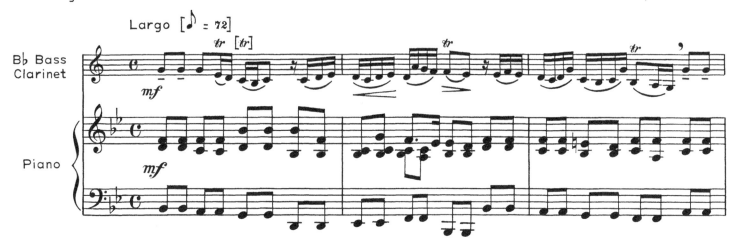

Romance and Troika
from Lieutenant Kijé Suite

SERGE PROKOFIEFF
Arr. by Herman A. Hummel

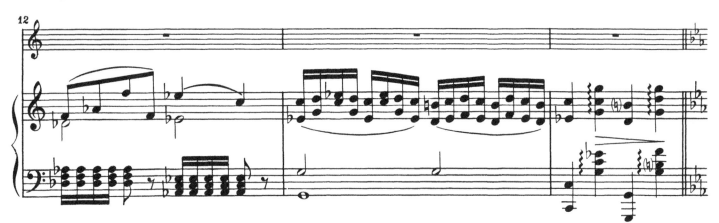

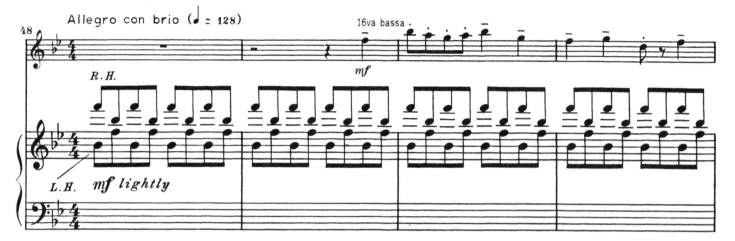

Divertissement in B♭

F. J. HAYDN
Transcribed by R. Hervig

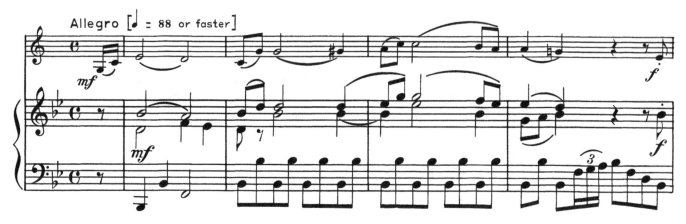

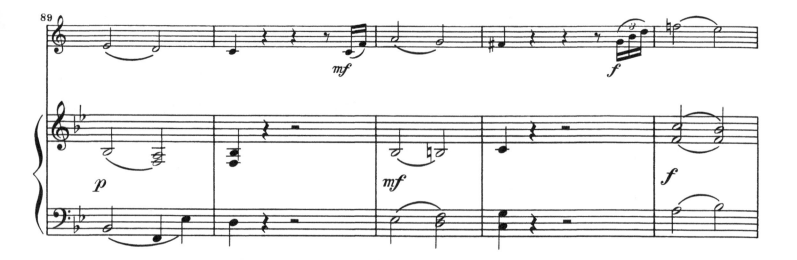

Concertino in D Minor

LEROY OSTRANSKY

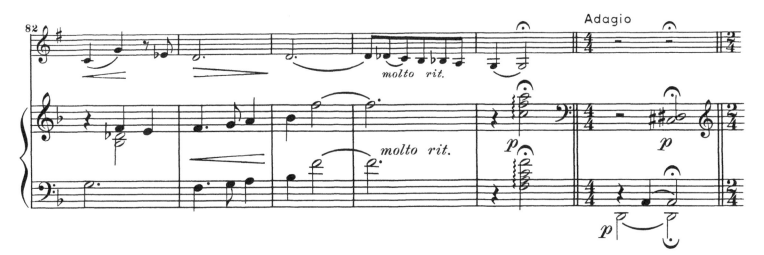

Sonatina

RICHARD HERVIG

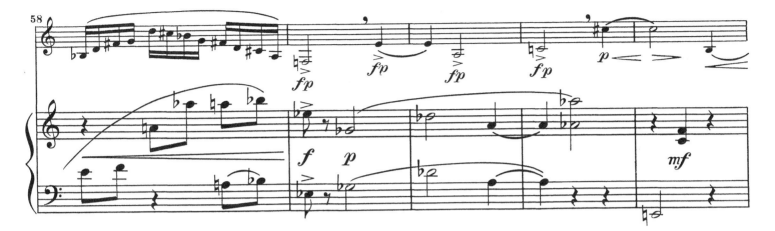

Chincoteague

CLARENCE E. HURRELL

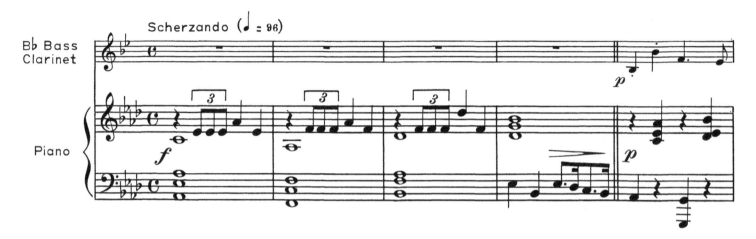

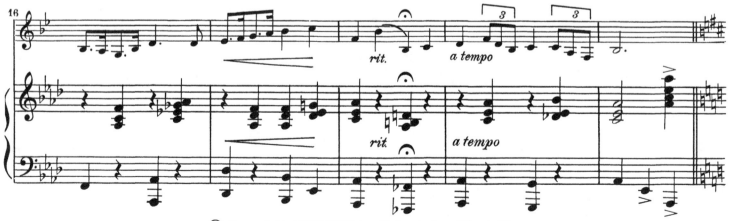

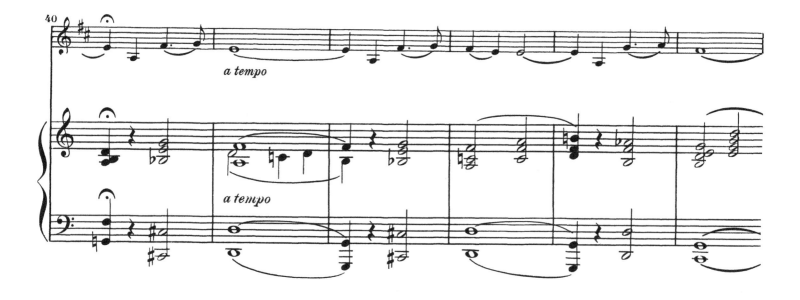

a tempo

a tempo

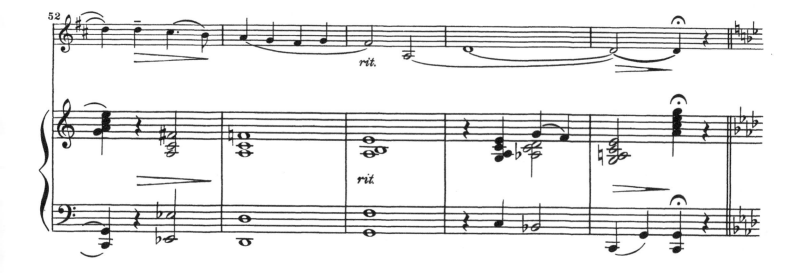

rit.

rit

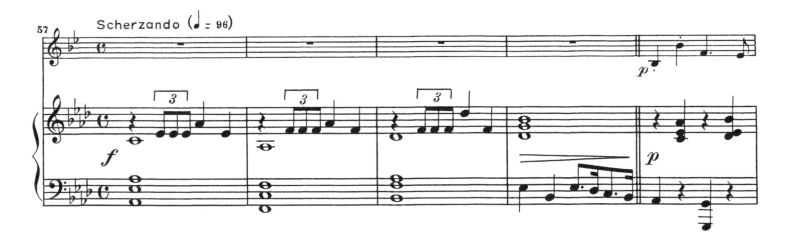

Andante
from Concerto in Bb Major

A. BEON
Transcribed by H. Voxman

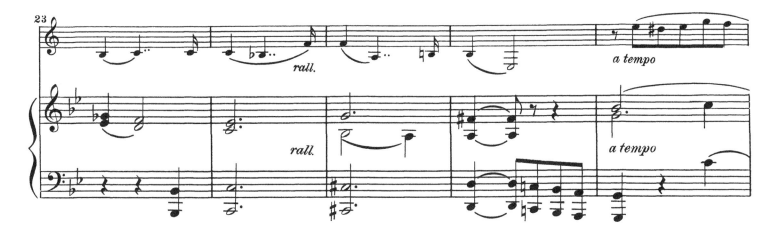

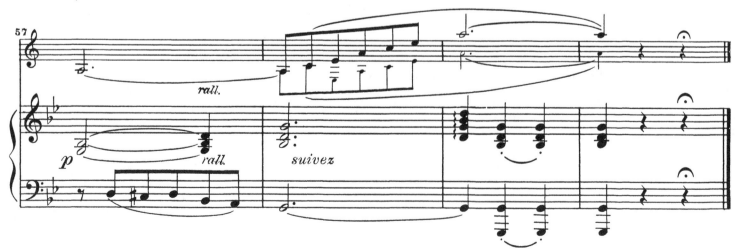